Moonlight Till Dawn

Jeanne Buesser

Dedicated to my sisters,

Tia and Laura

Table of Contents

Prologue

A new journey…
This is my second book of published poetry. I have found that poetry is one way that I have been able to heal from the multiple losses in my life.

For those of you who have not read my first book,Journey From Darkness to Light…, I had some wonderful years growing up in Kenya, East Africa, while my father set up a school, while my mother taught at the international school. I was challenged by being different when I came back to the United States as a teen.

I married a wonderful man and had two children and then the older one, my son, Danny died suddenly from cancer. My first book of poems comes from that loss. Our second and third sons both have special needs and needed ongoing therapy and careful attention.

My husband, Ray, died suddenly in January, 2010 at age 49. This book contains the writing which came from the grief of that loss.

The first thoughts after his death: How was I going to get through this?

I buried my oldest son 15 years ago, and now my husband? All my emotions came back, shock, loss, an overwhelming feeling that now I am all alone raising my sons.

Crying in my bed many nights missing him, knowing it all was on my shoulders. I had no backup plan. I always believed that your partner was with you for life when you got married. At 48, now a widow.

I had called my family doctor and told her about Ray passing away. She prescribed a low dose valium for me. I went to the pharmacy just holding on and met another recent widow, emotionally and physically drained.

She was a few years more down the road who filled my order, few years younger than I. We became friends exchanged emails and talked.

Going into Kmart and seeing Valentine's Day things displayed, a few weeks after the funeral. It broke my heart, I cried. I just made it home and took a valium. I wanted cards and candy, but knew I wasn't going to get any from him. I went to my Facebook page and cried while I changed my status from married to widow.

Soon after the funeral we had a major snowstorm with a lot of snow. It was so hard to get up and realize that I had to shovel the snow myself, I had no backup. I put gasoline in the snow blower and started it up. Some of the neighbors helped, when they could. Where before, Ray would have gotten up and done that earlier in the morning.

It snowed again that week and my sons helped to clear the driveway. I was using the snow blower in the back yard patio clearing it out and I heard a noise. I had scooped up the black rubber foot mat in the blades!!

I cursed out myself because now I couldn't use it!! God, I felt like an idiot. It was jammed tight. I'd forgotten it was there under the snow near the back door! My neighbor took out his tools and thank god it didn't damage the machine, but it took many hours until the whole mat was out. I won't do that again.

I started going to a therapist to help me through my grief very soon after, and the boys went to one also. I needed help to stand up again.

My middle son had started doing art lessons privately in 9th grade but stopped after 10th grade.

He is quite talented but only wanted to do art in high school not privately. I never had painted before so this was new to me, His art teacher became mine. It was fun but challenging learning how to blend colors. The painting lessons were once a week with other women artists. I began using his old paints and brushes, and really enjoyed it.

During that first year, I wrote poetry. I started drawing and doing artwork never doing it before this, and that's when I published a book on bullying children like mine, called He Talks Funny.

I decided to draw the cover of the book on paper. My art teacher helped me with pointers as I illustrated my first book, He Talks Funny. Then, I took a chance and started painting on paper for my first poetry book. Then the next one on canvas, for my 2nd poetry book cover. I have painted a few others for family members and friends.

Found a widow's website online. Please see the reference pages of this book. It was a life saver. Many times I was able to chat with people who had been through this, dealing with different subjects. It was a great website with various stages from very new to been there awhile and what challenges people went through, including their children, relationships.

And, then, after the first year, I was ready to start moving ahead again, with baby steps. Now I'm single!! How strange that felt. I didn't go out to bars and drink. How do I find out who I am again? It had been such a long since I was on the dating scene. It was scary looking online to see what people had written on their profiles.

A good friend recommended a great book on relationships which was out loud funny to read called What Smart Women Want.

It reminded me about the warning signs and do's and don'ts are you were meeting people on dates. It talked about these new relationships and how they could affect my kids.

I decided to go to the meetup.com website and start meeting others by joining groups. It was such a great feeling just going out for a good time, not having any pressure to date.

For the longest time it was so hard to listen to those people who were married, or divorced, who would talk about their husbands or ex-husbands when I didn't have one anymore.

It was bitter sweet. It was hard too because I now had to be a father and a mother. My kids needed a male mentor now, they didn't have one. I'm only sorry Ray didn't feel or see the positive influence he had on his kids.

The kids and I have survived nearly two years now. Ray's anniversary and his birthday came and went.

Other milestones came and went too, birthdays and holidays without him here to celebrate. And so I wrote poetry. I talked to him during long, lonely nights. I encouraged my kids and my family to tell stories about Ray.

My older son is now taking driver's ed at school. I only wish his dad was here to teach him. But instead he is watching over them both.

In my heart I know that when Danny died he wouldn't want me to give up but keep on living as hard as that was. The same goes for Ray.

Sometimes when a person carries a lot of baggage inside they can't see the forest for the trees.

Unless a person really talks about what they are feeling inside or their past (skeletons in the closet) you really don't know what is going on. Depression ran in his family.

Sometimes there are no signs shown so you don't know anyway when there is a problem. I guess I had some survivor guilt too.

I know I can't change things that have happened in the past with Ray but I know that they are both proud of me. Sometimes when major things happen it brings positive changes how people reach out in the extended family. Ray never celebrated his milestone birthday. I had a life celebration party at my house for family and friends after he passed away.

My birthday just passed, it was a milestone. My sons picked out such a wonderful card which said it all at the store. All I could do was hug and kiss them both. I'm so proud of them. My sister had a party celebration with my family and friends. It felt weird to celebrate mine, but I had a great time.

We just celebrated Thanksgiving. It felt strange with Ray not being here, too. I would have watched the parade in the morning on TV but we didn't do it this year. It was one of his favorite holidays, eating the turkey, and the trimmings, pies and watching the football game.

A good friend of mine came over to visit from out of state whom I haven't seen in a few years. We watched the last movies of him on TV.

This book takes the reader from the early days of my grief, soon after he left us until today when my sons and I have created a life for ourselves with new routines and new family history. I cry less but I miss him every day.

I hope that some of my words touch you and inspire you to also write your feelings if you've suffered a loss. I wish you healing and strength.

I would also like to thank Lisa, for her help with my editing of my books and Jennifer for doing my website. To those family and special friends old and new who have supported me in my journey, thank you. Jeanne can be contacted through her websites.

Jeanne Buesser

www.JeanneBuesser.com
www.ApraxiaNetwork.org
www.apraxianetworkofbergencounty@egroups.com
http://parentsptofview.blogspot.com/

The "Aha" Moment 3/30/12

I had been asking myself about this anchor of weight chained to my heart, stopping me from going ahead. I finally realized it was my past that I was afraid of letting go. That clothes I had stored Ray's and Danny's I didn't have to keep anymore. I donated them. The memories are in my head and heart. My kids didn't want Ray's clothes or liked them I asked and donated them. My heart felt good and lifted. Something so simple that I had made so hard for myself wasn't all these years. I had put the material clothes to the person who had them and held them to something that wasn't there. I was the person stopping myself. I was ready to let it all go.

Poems

Love - 11/30/03

What is Love?
Love is a delicate as a newborn's skin,
Renewing as the morning dew
Warm as sunshine,
Love is laughter in your heart.
A setting sunset
A deepest chasm
A never ending sea
A silent tear
The tide's ebb and flow
That is what love is to me.

Father's Day - 6/6/05

What is a father, just a man?
No. It is a husband who helps
raise a child to learn and grow,
To teach lessons too.
A father fills himself with pride
As he watches his offspring.
Then something happens, and
a child is gone, without warning.
What is a father to do?
He is expected to hold down the fort,
What of his pain?
He keeps it inside well hidden, He
longs for the child, but goes on.
He doesn't see that the child now
looks out for him. When before
He looked out after the child.

Ray - 2/16/10
(Two weeks after you left...)

Ray, as I shovel freshly fallen show, I think of how
you'd be here doing it.
You and Danny are watching me now.
I hope I make you proud as I raise our sons alone.

The Walk - 3/18/10

As I walk slowly along this road, my heart feels heavy
with a new load, of new found fears and an future
unknown I walk this road alone without my spouse to
hold my hand, to keep me falling on no demand.
To raise my sons without him here, and by myself I
sometimes fear. But he is watching me as I trudge
along, slowly singing a lonely song.

The Circle - 6/4/10

What is a circle? A continuous line without end.
Unknown prior events draw us together.
What adventures and journeys we take and teach others
helping us all.
Like life, we sometime don't know the rhyme nor reasons,
yet our souls are enriched by what has happened. We
become a different person, bearing the scars and then we
move on.

The Walk in the Meadow - 6/10/10

As I walk slowly through the field of long grasses,
A Maple tree, big and strong stands ahead.
Below its large branches, a bench where you both wait
patiently for me.
Though my visit there is very short, it brings a tear to my eyes.
Missing and knowing I'll see you both again when my time is
near, and I'll stretch my wings toward the sky.

Questions - 6/17/10

A friend the other day, asked me why I was so strong
anyway, "I have to be for the kids" I replied.
This emotional wall which we build up inside, is it a
blessing or a curse?
Someplace to hide, to find oneself and start over again,
when you're falling apart at the seams.
Who will hold me up when I fall, and will the strength to
climb back up on the beam.

Thinking of You - 11/7/10

Past memories suppressed hard to bring up,
was it so long ago when you were here?
Barely 9 months ago and time is going by so fast.

As days fly by and nights go past.
You not holding my hand, but I still fear.
Raising the boys along with no book to tell me,
 If I am doing okay or not.

Birthdays and holidays come and go but your
missed so much do you know?
In spite of it all I have no regrets of being your
spouse. Even though I cry.

I'll try to make you proud. With love from the heart.
We will meet again someday and never part.
You'll watch over me and the boys. Though I don't
know you're there, as I pray for strength in the cool
night air.

The Tide - 3/1/11

The tide is turning, I feel it in my bones,
The weight is lifting, the dark clouds parting.
A new dawn approaches, promising change.

Events are happening, dreams are coming to
fruition. Prayers are being answered.
Recognition here at last.
The long wait is over. My new journey begins.....

The Gate in the Courtyard - 3/8/11

A picture hangs on the wall, two people walk through a gate in
a courtyard. My journey's different now, "the gate beckons to
me. "Push me open," it invites, "and go through to the path
beyond" … A new journey.

I take a deep breath and put one foot in front of the other.
What past darkness is left behind. I go forth to the light,
moving on....

Reflections - 3/16/11

I tossed and turned; didn't sleep much at all,
talked out loud to the sturdy wall.
Thought about what you told me in spirit today...
Your dark past hidden inside, so afraid and painful
nowhere to hide.
A secret held for so long took its toll and darkened your soul,
suffocating your light. You never spoke about what happened.

I never knew.
It brought a weight too hard to bear, and broke your spirit.
It broke my heart to hear it told.
Hard and helpless your precious soul lived with pain so long,
never telling your story, Just trying to go along....

The Heart - 3/18/11

My heart was heavy but no more.
The weight has shifted, gone from sight.
The burden gone, no more sorrow, no more fright.
Love now enters, my light renewed.
Joy an old buried friend, returns.
I feel both of you near me now.
The dark clouds have parted to show
A beautiful rainbow and a brand new day.

A Friend 8/18/11

A friend is someone who is connected to your heart,
They lift you up when you fall apart,
The bond never broken is there for all time,
To love and cherish in your heart and mind.

The Cove 8/9/11

The cove is quiet and still.
Waters gently lap the shore.
Sun already risen warms the sky.
Pale blue color shows the day.
Another day has begun....
Birds already risen have flown away.
Street is empty, few cars drive by..
I sit and listen to the world awake.

Boat Ride - 8/10/11

Boat cuts through the water like a knife,
I'm holding the rail the breathtaking sight,
No sounds or birds are in the air,
Gentle wind whips my hair.
Slightly chilled, laughing with a friend by my side
We watch the sunset, enjoy the ride.

Three Birds - 8/11/11

Three birds in a nest weather the storms,
Trying their best to keep warm,
Through thick and thin they huddle together,
Watching out for each other in all sorts of weather,
Being so cheerful and smiling inside,
Braving the winds enjoying the ride.

The Night - 8/9/11

Deep blue water is the night sky with
lights that twinkle showing us the way,
We pick out the constellations and talk as we
walk by pulling the dogs on a quiet night.

A Summer Night - 7/27/11

Walking on a summer night as sunset leaves and dusk
arrives.
Summer sounds are in the air, planes, birds as the sky light
changes into night.
Darkness approaches, sunset rays no more on the horizon.
Blue gray sky begins to show, the moon peaks it's face into
the sky,
Birds outside quiet down, the world's asleep and peaceful.

Patterns - 7/18/11

Patterns like old habits woven into our lives, rugs, worn and
frayed. Pulling out old patterned yarns to make new ones.

Changing the way we think and act. Realizing the way some
things we'd done didn't work. Not seeing the lesson then.
Throwing our energy to the wind without getting the return flow
back. Thinking from the head and not the heart.

Feeling exhausted inside, no new fuel to keep the drive going.
I heard my voice say "stop" inside my head. How long
has it been? Helping others first? I'd forgotten about my own
needs fueling my fire. I finally listened and heard it.

Knowing now I can't pull everyone's weight.
Must let go, of this anchor.
Others saw what I didn't see. I couldn't accept
the change I had to make inside myself. Reaching for
something that I hadn't answered myself until now.

Your Favorite Song - 9/7/11

Hearing your favorite song on the cd,
grips my soul, forgiving you.
Tears run down my face out of control,
understanding the words hearing what they say.
Feeling sad I couldn't take your pain away.
Knowing how you felt now, like sand against the tide
washing away your strength while you cry inside.

Messages - 9/22/11

What messages are there in life's journeys?
Stops, starts and hesitation?
Different and difficult decisions on what paths we take.
Always asking questions, looking for answers
only finding them when you listen to your heart.

Ripples - 10/5/11

A pebble is thrown into the water. It sinks to the bottom never to be seen again.
But, where it enters the surface ripples appear almost invisible at first, then slowly they branch out on a endless plane.

Like the ripples we don't know how much influence we have to make a difference from one circumstance. Or don't always see the changes that happen or take place.

Music - 10/1/11

Music soothes the soul,
Brings joy to the heart.
Giving life meaning and direction.
Taking away sorrow and pain.
Restoring peace

The Moon - 10/5/11

Silently the moon rises over the water, sending its shimmering reflection upon the gentle waves below.

On this clear night you hear the waves lapping at the jetty, whilethe moon shines its light for all to see.

Energy - 10/5/11

Energy is around us all.
We move together in a circle as one.
Each of us swaying like palm trees in a breeze, passing
It along.

New Faces - 10/16/11

New faces making friends,
sharing stories turning a bend.
New adventures laughing around, good time ahead.
What next can be found?
Making cracks in my outside wall,
letting light in having a ball.

The Morning Light - 10/19/11

It's 6am dark outside. Fog is heavy like a blanket
of snow, Hard to see.
Like a ghost it hangs around, slowly lifting off the ground.
The dawn approaches it is first light. Away goes the fog into
the light.

Meadow Grasses -10/26/11

Meadow grasses sway to the movement of the wind.
Gracefully and silently like a golden river.

She - 11/2/11

Who is she?
Standing on a sandy beach feeling the energy of the world
around her.

Who is she?
A tree bending in the wind, moving to the pulsing rhythm of the
ocean.

Who is she?
Holding a ball of energy as she moves from side to side,
opening up herself to the universe.
She is me.

Breathing - 11/24/11

Energy flowing into my heart opening and closing like a flower.
Bringing me to a higher place.
My body rising on a floating pad remembering you...
Like it was yesterday.

Time - 11/27/11

Time changes all things, thoughts, bodies, minds in all of us.
What we thought was safe isn't.
What fears we had are now here.
We are forced to take steps on paths we didn't choose.
They're unexpected changes as we go ahead. Time moves
forward though we try and hold it back.

Candle - 11/30/11

Each of us is a candle with light glowing inside. Spreading
warmth and friendship to the world. We give light to the
darkest reaches of our souls.
Showing it a path to follow, making a difference one day at a
time.

Light - 1/9/12

Light enter my heart so it can flow,
meaning and direction come to show me the way.
Pain can subside and memories return.
So I can get through this day.
Water- Wash down my body and cleansing my soul - releasing
my pain, restoring peace.

The Truth 1/18/12

Old feelings never shown always buried long time ago,
Never dealt with hidden from view.
Break down my walls really feel my pain.
Release myself from wishes I never knew.
Holding onto things that weren't there- bringing me down.

The Bridge - 1/23/12

There are some bridges yet to cross, some sturdy, some not.
Yet once crossed, I cannot turn back. Must go on...

Renewing my energy and finding myself as I travel this path.
Realizing who I am embracing it, not judging others and
forgiving them.

Insights - 2/2/12

I had directed my blame towards others first before realizing
that I had to take responsibility for my own actions. That there
were faults in our relationship that we didn't know how to deal
with letting them go on.

Looking back now, I see my pain and hurt not addressed
by me but hidden away. Now coming to the surface again
I must face it.

Loving and forgiving myself for things I did, and didn't do.
Learning who I am, human, not invincible. Accepting my
talents and faults together in a proper balance will bring
me peace.

Driftwood - 2/15/12

Driftwood pieces float on the open sea,
They are lost past emotions and are part of me.
Different sizes crash upon the shore.
Raw and painful, I'm denying them once more.
Unlock the door and go inside until I resolve them all.
My heart opened up wide, so I can cry, heal and not fall.

If - 3/10/12

If things had been different a long time ago between you and
me.
Would our relationship have grown or was it just a fantasy?
I have thought of you often over the years you see.
I've wondered if you'd remember me?

The fun times we had dancing at the 92nd St "Y ",
and you by my side.
Staying up late then saying long goodbyes.

Sorrow -3/12/12

When you see a loved one's minds and bodies begin to fade,
the memories lost never replayed.
Realization to never being the same,
so sad no control begins the game.
What once they knew nevermore
to be talked about can't open that door.
We all grow older yet forget our ages and the times
of happier days, and other rhymes.

Hollow Halls- 4/19/12

Hollow halls echo in the mind, bringing back our memories
that are kind.
Childhood and older memories once here are no more.

Laughter, playing in the rooms, growing up I look at the floor.
Items, furniture gone an empty house remains. Our footsteps
echo as we walk these halls never to set foot in them again. A
door closes, a new chapter….

Things changed but not forgotten. These hollowed halls have
their stories to tell.

Ghosts -4/9/12

Remembering better times as we sit down at the table...
Ghosts from our pasts remain.
Bittersweet the realization of the present we can't go back
again.

Knowing things aren't the same, time goes much to fast.
Can't change what is here now how it just won't last.
Like a flicker of light here and now a spark remains behind.
But to keep it lit we have to remember the memories for all
time.

Blue Heron- 6/6/12

Standing still watching the world go by,
a lone blue heron in a marsh awaits.
The gentle wind ruffles its long blue feathers.
Slowly moves forward blinking his black eyes watching for
motion.
Magestic is he like a mountain river flowing to the sea.

Tributes to Friends and Family Who Left Us Too Soon

Tribute to Joey 9/01
(Joseph) 1963-1987

Joey,

I think about you a great deal lately, especially when I hear classical music. I remember how you beautifully played those pieces and how music filled the air. Your fingers glided over the piano keys. Your passion about the 20's and 30's and how you loved to hear old melodies, reflected the music scene back then. How sophisticated you were. I remember you loved antiques.

Though two years younger than I, you were like the brother I never had. I shall always cherish the memories. I'm sure you're playing music in heaven for the angels. I'm sure you've met Danny. I told your mom long ago you were a very special person who was too good for this earth!

In memory of Randi - 5/01
1958-2001

Randi, when you walked into the room, it filled with warmth and sunshine. No one was a stranger. Everyone felt at home in your presence. You showed that the world can be a beautiful place. You will be missed surely, and never forgotten. You inspire all!

Randi's 1st anniversary - 3/02

I saw you in December for my mom's birthday. Your beaming smile on your face glowed. We were talked about what business aspects I might pursue. You had a heart of gold and a spirit that included everyone. You accomplished things that other people wouldn't have dreamed to do, ventured to places not many people would go. You will always be remembered.

Nancy - 11/11

Nancy, like your sister before you, a beacon of light.
Righting the wrongs, making them right.
Not looking back at all you've done,
But going ahead like the blazing sun.

Susan A Tribute to a Friend - 7/02
1960- July, 22, 2002

We worked together many years ago when we were young.
You walked into the classroom with your family. We met
again, we reminisced about old times, rekindled the friendship.
I will never forget your smile and kind heart. I will reach out to
Bob, Taryn, and Robyn. You'll be missed. I
know you're watching over them from above.
Your friend, Jeanne

My Tribute to Margie – 12/03

I really didn't know you well, but you were a special
person I could tell, since two children and your husband
had passed away. I invited you to have dinner at
thanksgiving at my mom's . We were glad to have you
there. A stranger who had no place to go. You were
thankful for each day. You smiled, laughed and gave
great advice on how to live, never thinking twice. On
how many lives you changed. You will be missed.

Sandee - 2/21/12

You loved life it shown in your eyes, always kind and
thoughtful to all.
After meeting you in person, I could see how he'd fell in love
with you and under your spell. You were an inspiration to
many more I could tell. You're sadly missed by us all,
But I'm sure where you are...... having a ball.

Donna - 2/21/12

Your laughter was contagious, and so were you... Happy and
helping other that is always true. You touched so many people
I'm not so sure you're aware...

How you'll never be forgotten and how much we all did care.
Even when it was very hard when I visited you .
Some things you said to me...
My son and I will hold your memory in our hearts lovingly.

Anne - 2/21/12

The last matriarch of dad's family, you lived a wonderful life.
One whom I'd never met, but always
were talked about and looked up to by him all the time.
It was nice to hear how busy and happy you were.
When I got your letter addressed to me, my heart was broken inside.
It comforted me and I realize . How strong you were without support all those years ago.... Raising your son alone against the tide....

My Special Friend - 9/21/07

You were a very special friend, never asking for anything
But giving all the love you had though you never spoke.
You connected to my soul, knew my thoughts and worries,
you listened regardless of what I talked about.
You were the daughter I never had, even with
your four legs.
There for me during my worst times you put up with everything.
I hope now you are happy and at peace.
I will always miss you

Website Resources

Also check out local papers for other support groups in your town, therapists, hospitals.

(a new jersey database that list disorders by area and other support groups). Njgroups.org

Meetups.com

40's and 50's widows and widowers group in Bergen County
http://www.meetup.com/Young-widows-widowers-of-Bergen-County/

Young Widows.widowers support groups online
http://www.ywbb.org/forums/ubbthreads.php

Made in the USA
Charleston, SC
02 August 2012